Writer's Bites:
Topics You Can Sink Your Teeth Into

Writing & Publishing Terminology
for Romance Writers

by Maggie Worth

Writing & Publishing Terminology for Romance Writers
Copyright 2013 Maggie Worth

Copyright 2013 Maggie Worth
Cover art by April Saunders

ISBN-13: 978-1490933887
ISBN-10: 1490933883

Introduction

A couple of years ago, I decided to get off my duff and start writing the novel I'd been talking about for years. I knew I had a lot to learn and, since I'm the kind of person who likes to understand how things work, I talked a friend into attending a writer's conference with me so I could figure things out. To be honest, I thought I'd have a head start since I'd been writing professionally for almost two decades. Ha! Right! No such luck. Fiction – and especially romance fiction, which is what I write – has a complex set of rules and terminology all its own.

The first thing I discovered is that there are about a million subgenres within the dozen or so well-known genres. Who knew? Apparently I should have, because people kept asking what I wrote. By lunchtime on day one, I'd perfected a concise and honest answer: "Uh, I dunno." That got a lot of laughs, mainly because everyone's been there at some point. Maybe you're there now. If so, don't fret. You're perfectly normal.

I'm pretty hard to overwhelm, but that first day almost did it. I went to bed early and just stared at the ceiling, my head spinning with new phrases, familiar words that had suddenly gained new meanings, and overheard conversations that sounded something like this:

Writer 1: "My WIP is killing me. The story arc isn't matching the character arcs, my subplot is leading nowhere, and I don't know how I'm going to get to the HEA."

Writer 2: "What subgenre?"

1: "CatRom. Regency."

2: "I don't know how you do that. My voice is wrong and I can't write third. I always end up head-hopping."

1: "POV shifts are easy for me, but scene/summary is a whole other matter."

2: "I hear you. I guess we just keep doing our daily words and look for some craft workshops."

1: "But I'm pitching today! What if I get a request for full?"

2: "Big Six or E?"

1: "I'm hoping for New York."

2: "You'd better skip the sessions and BICHOK."

I was utterly baffled. Were HEA and HFN new cable networks? Was Writer 1 working on a feline love story? Did Writer 2 really want to do devotionals and learn to make macramé owls? Frustration, confusion, despair! I mean, the conversation makes perfect sense to me now, but back then it sounded like maximum-security governmental pig Latin. Let me tell you, by the end of day three, I had a phenomenally solid grasp on how much I didn't know.

So I started researching, reading, and asking a ton of questions. Eventually I managed to write a book, but then I had to figure out how to pitch it. More research. 'cause guess what? Every publisher has different submission guidelines and each agent is looking for different kinds of stories. And there's this evil thing called a "synopsis" that everyone requires. Once the book sold, I had to interpret the contract terms and editorial letter and then get through a dozen rounds of revisions with more types of editors than I knew existed. Plus cover art, marketing, accounting… The list really does go on and on. Finally, the book was published. Done with the learning curve, right? Uh-uh. Promotion, reviewing, and royalties all have their own lingo. And you generally have to learn it while scrambling to write book two.

Sound awesome? The writing is. The experience is. Learning how to bring characters to life, to make your dialog sparkle and your story flow? That's amazing. Figuring out your personal process is arduous, but immensely rewarding. Getting your very first royalty check is about the coolest thing ever, even if it only buys you a small raspberry mochaccino. If you love writing, it's worth every ounce of hard work and every moment of insanity.

But those first few weeks (or months, or years) of trying to learn the acronyms and master the vocabulary? That part's just not fun. At all. It's confusing and frustrating and mind-numbing. And just when you think you've heard it all, something else whams you out of left field. Plus, not everyone is comfortable butting in on conversations between perfect strangers to ask what the heck they just said. Yet knowing how to talk about your craft, your industry, and your genre is truly important. It allows you to communicate with your peers, helps you figure out the fun stuff, and gives you credibility with agents and editors.

And that's why I wrote this book. You need to learn the language, but it can be more manageable for you than it was for me. You can learn from my mental pain and suffering and from the confusion and anguish of those who taught me. Lucky you!

Understand that this isn't an utterly comprehensive list. It can't be. Many regions and groups have unique language quirks and, as you probably know, the publishing industry is in the midst of a major revolution, so new acronyms crop up all the time. It's also not an in-depth look at any one term. I'll be exploring specific topics in further Writers' Bites books, but starting with vocabulary is always a good thing. This book should give you the kind of solid, broad-based foundation many of us wish we'd had when we were starting out.

Before we get into the nitty gritty, let's start with the most important definition in this entire book:

Writer – person who writes. This is you.

Note that the definition is not "person who is published" or "person with a professional writing degree." Yes, those people are writers. But if you are serious about learning your craft and you've put pen to paper or tapped out a story on your keyboard, you are a writer, too.

Get that definition through your head now. Recite it in front of a mirror if you have to. Because until you master it, none of the rest matters.

Welcome to the wild and wacky world of writing. We're glad you're here.

About Writer's Bites

Writer's Bites is a series of short, topic-focused books designed to help writers attack and master one facet of the writing craft or publishing industry at a time. Each book breaks the focus subject into approachable, digestible parts and includes examples, tips, advice, and suggestions for real-life use and practice.

Virtual Curtsies

I am immensely blessed to have amazing critique partners: Cheryl with her eagle eye for a misplaced comma, Kim for her fresh perspective and enthusiasm and Trish for accompanying me to that first convention and being my number one cheerleader ever since.

Unending gratitude goes out to my cover artist, April Saunders, who keeps me sane at our day job and who has patiently listened to many a long, uninteresting monologue about my writing and grad school dilemmas over chips and salsa.

Many thanks also to everyone who thought this series was a good idea and to the myriad individuals, groups, websites, blogs, books, and articles from which I learned all these terms in the first place.

Acceptance – when an agent or publisher agrees to represent or publish your book. You want this. Acceptance may come via phone, e-mail, or letter.

Acceptance on Proposal – when an agent or publisher agrees to represent or publish your book based only on a proposal as opposed to a manuscript. This is the norm for non-fiction works (including articles for magazines). In the fiction world, however, most publishers want a full. Once you begin selling well, you may be able to send proposals to your existing publisher or agent.

Acceptance Rate – percentage of submissions that are accepted for publication. This rate varies between genres and even between subgenres. Different sources also report vastly differing rates. The acceptance rate for small and electronic publishers is usually much higher than the rate for the big New York houses; most sources do not include self-published works or those published through a vanity press. In fiction, the reported acceptance rate ranges between about one and seven percent.

Acknowledgement – short passage in which the author thanks an individual who supported or assisted in the writing of the book. Acknowledgements are usually grouped together at the beginning of the book in a section known, appropriately enough, as the "Acknowledgement Section." When acknowledging professional sources, such as doctors, coroners, museum curators, etc., it is courteous to ask how the individual prefers to be acknowledged. (Also see credit.)

E.g.: Doctor Bob Jones or Robert. M. Jones, M.D. or Robert Jones, Doctor of Podiatry

Acquiring Editor – editor at a publishing house who is responsible for reading submissions and determining which books should be offered contracts. Depending on the size and policy of the house, these editors may or may not work with authors after acceptance. In larger houses, acquiring editors often have assistants who read all submissions first to narrow the pool.

Action Tag – sentence, usually short, that precedes or follows a line of dialog and demonstrates an action on the part of the speaker. Action tags are useful for indicating the speaker and for showing state of mind or physical actions. They also help avoid excessive use of "said," and are generally stronger and less intrusive than using an adverb or a said alternative.

E.g.: She peered at me as though trying to assess my honesty, then her shoulders slumped "Thank God."

Active Voice – when the subject of a sentence is acting rather than being acted upon. Opposite of passive voice and generally preferred for fiction writing, except when placing emphasis, such as on a character's powerless state.

> E.g.: <u>Pam kicked</u> the door shut. (See also passive voice.)

Advance – payment received before any copies of your book sell. Advances are sometimes distributed on a pre-arranged schedule. For example, you might receive a portion upon acceptance and another portion upon delivery of a completed manuscript. You will not begin to receive royalty payments until you earn out. It's important to note that some books – particularly those that are e-published – do not receive advances.

Advance Publicity – publicity, such as advertising, social media marketing, etc., that occurs before your book is published. Publisher and author opinions differ, both about the effectiveness of advance publicity and about the proper strategy. Most agree that social media, blogging, and other types of marketing can be extremely useful, but advance paid advertising might be best suited for established authors and celebrity authors.

Advance Reader – person, most often a professional reviewer or published author, who reads your book after you and your editor have finished all edit rounds, but before the book is published, usually to create advance publicity.

Advance Reader Copies – copies of your finished manuscript that are sent out before your book is published, usually to review sites or to published authors who may plug your book. Often called ARCs (pronounced as one word like "arks").

Adverb – part of speech that modifies a verb. Adverbs usually end in "ly." Most editors agree that adverbs should be used sparingly. When you find an adverb in your manuscript, consider simply using a stronger verb instead.

> E.g.: Betty walked <u>quickly</u> to the door. (You might replace with "Betty rushed to the door.")

Agency Clause – publisher contract clause that requires you to indicate your agent and describes the way in which your publisher will interact with your agent.

Agent – professional who specializes in pitching books to and negotiating deals with publishers on behalf of an author.

Agent Contract – contract between you and your agent. Your contract will describe your working relationship, including your responsibilities, the agent's responsibilities, and the agent percentage.

Agented – term for an author who is represented by an agent. Some publishers will specify that they accept "agented submissions only."

Agent Percentage – percentage of your advance and royalties paid to your agent for representing your book and negotiating your contract.

Alpha Hero – hero with alpha male qualities.

Alpha Male – male character who displays typical Alpha behaviors: strength, assertiveness, overt masculinity, blatant sexuality, confidence, power, dominance (not necessarily in the sense of BDSM), leadership, swift decision-making, and a tendency to claim partners rather than romance them. Extremely popular in the romance genre, these heroes may cross lines to aggression and arrogance, though you must always assign them a redeeming quality to give the reader a reason to engage. The term is derived from traditional wolf pack hierarchy. (See also beta male.)

Amazon Author Central – area of Amazon devoted to you as an author. You can create and edit your author profile from this page as well as see sales ranking history, author rank, reviews, and more. This is not a public area and is password-protected.

Amazon Author Page – page on the Amazon site that includes your author profile, picture, list of books, etc. You need to populate this page once you have a book on Amazon.

Amazon Author Rank – system established by Amazon in 2012 that ranks authors against one another in terms of sales. Ranks are subdivided by genre and appear on your Amazon Author Central page.

Amazon Rank – may refer to an Amazon Author Rank or Amazon Sales Rank.

Amazon Sales Rank – Amazon ranking system that compares the sales of your book to the sales of all other books in your category (electronic or print and paid or free).

Amnesiac in the Storm – one of the classic romance tropes. The hero or heroine turns up in a storm or washes up on a beach with no recollection of who he or she is. Variations include full or partial amnesia due to airplane or car accidents, war, illness, or injury.

Antagonist – person who plots against your hero and/or heroine or makes it difficult for them to achieve their goals.

Sometimes called the villain. In a mystery or suspense, this is most likely the killer/stalker/etc. (See also protagonist.)

Anthology – collection of works, most often novellas, poems, or short stories, that are published together as one book. The individual works are usually related in some way and may be written by one author (single-author anthology) or by many (multi-author anthology). In multi-author anthologies, the authors share all advances and royalties according to the contract terms.

AP Style – short for "Associated Press," this is the style in which most news articles are written. Lifestyle magazines typically use a slightly modified version. This is also the style used for most press releases. Updated periodically, the AP Style Guide is available through most booksellers and libraries should you need it.

Arbitration – binding negotiation conducted by a neutral third party that takes place in lieu of court proceedings. Arbitration clauses appear in many agent and publishing contracts. By signing such a contract, you agree that you will be bound by the arbiter's decision in the event of a contract dispute between you and your agent or publisher.

ARC – see advance reader copy.

Archetype – recognizable character type that occurs across literature. Classical examples include the Hero, the Wise Old Man/Woman, the Damsel in Distress, and the Trickster. Romance examples include the Best Friend, the Bad Boy, the Librarian, the Warrior, and the Free Spirit.

Art Department – publishing house department responsible for cover art. This department may also work with marketing to design promotional materials such as ads, fliers, etc.

ASIN – stands for Amazon Standard Identification Number. This number is assigned to everything sold on Amazon. For books, the ASIN is usually the same as the ISBN.

Auction – situation in which two or more publishers (or film/television producers) are bidding for the rights to your book. This generally means your contract will be more favorable, either in terms of royalties or in terms of other concessions, such as advance copies and promotional support.

Audio Book – version of your book converted to a playable media format such as a CD or MP3. This allows readers to listen to your book in the car, on their MP3 players, on the computer, or through audio-enabled e-readers.

Audio Rights – the right to record and sell your book in audio book format. These rights may be specified in your initial contract or sold later; your audio rights might be owned by an entity other than your print publisher.

Audit – process in which a professional accountant reviews figures and calculations to ensure accuracy. For a writer, this usually has two forms. In the first, the author requests an audit of her agent's or publisher's accounting records to verify that sales figures and royalty payments have been computed and distributed properly. In the second, the Internal Revenue Service audits your taxes to make sure you didn't under-report your earnings or over-report your deductions and that you paid the right amount of tax.

Audit Clause – contract clause that specifies how often you may request an audit of your account and the process all such audits must follow. This may appear in your publisher contract and/or your agent contract.

Author – person who writes something. Yep, it really is that broad. You can author a vast array of things, including books, songs, letters, and agreements. In the publishing world, the term is used to differentiate between the person who wrote the book (author) and the publisher, editors, marketing writers, and others who write "stuff" related to your book.

Author Bio – your biography, as a writer. This usually includes publication credits, at least in summary, as well as other information such as hobbies, pets, organization memberships, and where you live. You'll probably have at least three bios: a short, a long, and a mini.

Author Brand – this is the image you want readers to have of you as an author. Physical representations of your brand might include a logo, a tagline, and/or specific symbols. It's important to understand, however, that these things are not your brand. They are what you use to communicate your brand to readers. Your brand is much more abstract. It's who you are, what you stand for, and how you write.

Author Branding – the process of creating and promoting your author brand.

Author Copies – electronic or physical copies of your final book that are provided to you at no charge by your publisher. These are yours to use for giveaways, contests, etc. You normally receive only a limited number of author copies and most contracts prohibit you from selling them.

Author Interference – the term used when what the author wants to say gets in the way of the story. Authors, publishers, agents, and readers all have vastly differing opinions about what constitutes author interference – and how much of it is desirable or permissible in a story.

Author Page – a page on an online bookseller's website that is dedicated to you and your books. It generally includes a list of your books including cover art, basic information, and customer reviews of each as well as your author bio. It might also include a blog feed or other extras. Author pages might also appear on review sites.

Author Profile – electronic profile that includes information about you as an author and, sometimes, a picture. These may appear on websites for online booksellers, review sites, your publisher's site, blogs, and other social media platforms.

Author Voice – see voice.

Avon – Avon Romance, a division of HarperCollins Publishers.

Babe – term for a physically perfect heroine. Babes generally need to come with other flaws or baggage in order to make them relatable and endearing to the average reader.

Back Cover – copy that is physically located on the back cover of your book. This usually includes a description of the story, including the hook, and may also include brief laudatory quotes from advance readers.

Backlist – all your previously published books. When a new reader finds and loves one of your new releases, you hope she will then go buy your backlist.

Back Story – history, particularly a character's history, that occurs prior to the beginning of your story. This might include where the character grew up, past relationships, etc. Ideally, back story should be woven in small doses throughout your book rather than told all at once at the beginning. Occasionally spelled as one word: "backstory."

Bag Sponsor – entity that pays money to have its logo or name printed on the giveaway bag at a conference or event. This can be a company (such as a publisher), organization, individual (such as a cover artist), or author. The term is also sometimes used to describe those who donate items (or money for items) to fill the bag.

Barriers – things that prevent the main character from reaching his or her goal. In a romance, this usually means issues that challenge your couple's relationship. These can be internal conflicts such as one character's fear of commitment or external conflicts such as distance. Most books – romance and otherwise – involve overcoming barriers.

BDSM – has three parts: (BD) = bondage and discipline; (DS) = dominance and submission; (SM) = sadism and masochism. Often written BDS/M.

Bestseller – book with top-ranking sales.

Beta – can mean "beta male," "beta hero," or "beta reader."

Beta Hero – hero with beta male qualities.

Beta Male – male character that is less aggressive than an Alpha male. Betas are generally attractive, intelligent, funny, and approachable. They are easygoing, but not pushovers and more sensitive than Alphas, but by no means feminine. They are more likely to romance a woman than to claim her and may hide trauma or heartbreak beneath an always-ready smile. Betas may be the hero or a secondary character and may have "alpha male moments."

Beta Reader – person who reads your manuscript once you feel it is ready for submission. Beta readers are usually unfamiliar with the story and may not be other writers. The idea is to get fresh, honest feedback from a reader perspective. The term "beta" refers to the fact that these readers are the second ones to read your manuscript, after your critique partner(s).

BICHOK – stands for butt in chair, hands on keyboard. In other words, the book won't write itself. The only way to get it done is to sit down and do it.

Big Misunderstanding – romance trope in which a couple is kept apart by a major misunderstanding on the part of one or both parties. Usually, the misunderstanding could be resolved by a simple conversation. For example, the heroine gets upset because she sees the hero having dinner with another woman, only to later find out that the "other woman" was his cousin/sister/client/lesbian ex-babysitter. This particular trope has largely fallen out of fashion.

Big Six – refers to the six major New York houses, all of which are considered traditional publishers, though they may have digital-first imprints. As of early 2013, the Big Six are Hachette, Macmillan, Penguin Group, HarperCollins, Random House, and Simon & Schuster.

Bio – short for "biography." See author bio.

Black Moment – see dark moment.

Bleak Moment – regional variation of "black moment."

Bloat – excess and unnecessary verbiage or information that weighs down your sentence, scene, or book. Bloat slows your story and should be cut.

Blog – short for "web log," though most people have probably forgotten that this is so. A blog is a place for you to interact with your readers by telling them what you're doing and sharing your viewpoints. Many authors use blogs to hold contests.

Blog Feed – location on a website or author page (other than your actual blog site) to which your blog automatically posts.

Blog Tour – promotional activity in which an author guest posts on several different blogs during a short span of time. The intent is to find new readership and create buzz, usually about a new release or other event.

Blurb – short summary of your story that includes your hook. Blurbs appear in catalogs and on the buy pages of online retailers. You will use a draft of your blurb first when pitching your book, and then a revised version later when guest posting or announcing a contest. You will probably write two or more blurbs of different lengths for different situations.

Bodice-ripper – particular type of romance that involves a high level of passion without the frank, clear language characteristic of erotica and erotic romance. The term arose from the 70s and 80s trend, particularly in historical romances, of depicting a disheveled heroine (often clasped in—or trying to escape from—a manly embrace) on the cover. "Bodice-ripper" is sometimes used to specifically describe stories in which the heroine is ravished rather than seduced and some, particularly those who aren't fond of the genre, simply use the term to mean any romance novel.

Boilerplate – standard verbiage at the end of a press release that describes the company, organization, or individual, and provides contact information or a link where the media can find additional details or reach a representative for comments. Major corporations use boilerplates, your publisher probably uses a boilerplate, and you should write one for yourself as well. Depending on your publisher, you may be permitted to use its boilerplate in addition to yours

Book – that thing you wrote or are writing. Once upon a time, a book was a bound, printed novel. Now, a book can be as short as novella-length and may be print or electronic.

Book Club – group of people who meet regularly, either in person or virtually, to talk about books. Most read and discuss one book at a time with all members reading the same work. Some book clubs also have speakers, book signings, and other events, which may create a promotional opportunity for you as an author.

Book Launch – flurry of publicity and promotion around the release of a book. Some authors throw physical or virtual book launch parties. Others go on blog or book signing tours.

Book-length Fiction – work of fiction long enough to be considered for print as an independent title (not as part of an anthology). In general, the industry uses 40,000 words as the benchmark, though some publishers print shorter books and others have a much higher word count requirement for print consideration.

Booklist – review journal used by most librarians to choose books to buy and recommend.

Bookmark – thingie that marks your place in a book. It sounds like an obvious term to define, but bookmarks are important because they remain a popular giveaway item among readers and authors alike—even if the book in question is available only in e-book format. Such bookmarks often include an image of one or more of your book covers, your author name, and other info. You may want to add a QR code and/or a list of your backlist titles (when you have one).

Book Proposal – document outlining your concept for a book, usually with extensive detail. This is the norm for submitting non-fiction work and may be an option for authors who have established a readership and relationship with their current publishers. Some fiction editors/agents consider a fiction proposal to be your query and partial.

Book Review – electronic or print write-up that provides an opinion on your book. Reviews often include short plot summaries along with the reviewer's feelings about the work. Most include a rating system and many include other information such as heat level, genre, etc. Reviews may be written on review sites, in magazines or newsletters, on blogs, or on online bookseller sites.

Bookseller – entity that sells books. Essentially, this means a book store and all the people who work in it. Booksellers may be online or brick-and-mortar outlets.

Book Signing – event at which an author signs copies of his or her book for readers. These may be held at booksellers, conferences, charity events, etc. and may be free or require the reader to make a donation or pay a small fee. Structure and regulations vary, but the idea is to gain publicity for your book as well as the store or organization holding the event. E-book authors sometimes sign cover slicks or other printed materials in lieu of physical books.

Boss and Secretary – romance trope that's exactly what it sounds like: a relationship between an employer and employee.

Breaking the Third (or Fourth) Wall – this happens when a character or narrator addresses the audience directly. It comes from theatre, in which actors called the invisible wall between the stage and the audience the third wall (or fourth wall, depending on how the stage was built). Opinions vary wildly about whether—and how often—breaking the wall is acceptable.

Brick-and-Mortar – physical location of a store or other business (as opposed to an online location or web store).

Buy Link – web link that takes readers to the specific page of an online bookseller's site from which your book can be purchased.

Buyer –bookseller or library employee responsible for buying books for resale or lending. You need these folks to stock print versions of your book.

Buzz – public relations term that means people are talking about something (preferably your book), either in person, on social media, or in the press.

C

C&D – see cease and desist.

Cardboard Characters – two-dimensional characters. These characters lack depth of emotion or motivation and the reader doesn't get a real sense of what the character is like, other than on a surface or physical level.

Category – see category romance.

Category Romance – romance novels that fit into a particular category or line within a major romance house. Examples include historical, cowboy, contemporary, romantic suspense, etc. Category romances generally follow a well-known formula, have strict writing rules, and often include popular tropes. Sometimes called series romance, they are generally shorter than single-title romance novels.

CatRom – short for category romance.

Cease & Desist – refers to a letter, print or electronic, instructing someone to stop doing something. In publishing, this usually means informing someone that they are quoting, selling, or otherwise using your trademarked material in an inappropriate way and that you want them to stop.

Celebrity Author – generally refers to writers who are already celebrities (socialites, actors, singers, etc.) The term may occasionally be used to describe an author so well known that he or she has become a celebrity (think James Patterson or Danielle Steele).

Chapter – can refer to a chapter of a book or to a sub-group of a national organization.

Character Arc – a character's journey of growth through a book or play. It usually follows the events and feelings that cause the character's opinion, feeling, or attitude on a particular topic to change.

Character Model – see character sketch.

Character Sheet – data sheet that lists a character's name, vital information, physical description, history, and other salient details such as job, education, etc. The purpose is to keep track of your character's information so you aren't constantly trying to remember things such as what color his eyes are.

Character Sketch – similar to a character sheet, but written in narrative rather than as a list of data.

Characterization – the creation of characters and the transmission of information, such as physical characteristics, preferences, quirks, and personality traits, about them. This includes ensuring that your character would actually take the actions you are assigning them—or using out-of-character actions to show growth, emotion, etc.

Chicago Manual of Style – style guide used by many publishing houses, sometimes with specific exceptions. Print versions of the guide are carried by most libraries and booksellers and online subscriptions are available. Often abbreviated CMOS.

Chick Lit – fiction genre that addresses common women's issues such as marriage and family, career, relationships, etc., and is characterized by humor and a very lighthearted tone. It can be, but is not always, a subgenre of romance.

Children's Literature – books for kids, as one might expect. Specifically, this refers to books that are not picture books, meaning text is more prevalent than pictures, and are intended for children under about age eight or nine. See also middle grades.

Clean Writing – writing that eliminates unnecessary words, descriptions, repetition, etc.

Cliché – overused phrase, word, characterization, or plot.

Closed Door – refers to action, usually sex, that occurs behind closed doors, meaning that the reader is not privy to the action.

CMOS – short for Chicago Manual of Style.

Co-author – author who writes a book in cooperation with you. Co-authors generally split the royalties according to a pre-determined agreement.

Coherence – the degree to which ideas, scenes, chapters, and actions flow into one another in a sensible, logical, and effective way.

Cold Reader – someone who reads your draft or manuscript with no (or at least limited) prior information about the plot, characters, etc. The point of a cold reader is to solicit an unbiased opinion on your work, particularly in terms of coherence and story.

Comma Splice – comma used to combine what should be two separate sentences into one. Not favored by editors. Use a semicolon or a period instead, please

> E.g.: She hoped John wasn't going to tell the whole story, Betsy was boring enough for both of them.

Commercial Fiction – refers to popular or genre fiction, which is theoretically created to be sold, as opposed to literary fiction, which is theoretically created purely for its own sake.

Conflict – any instance of ideals, emotions, attitudes, or desires in opposition.

Contemporary – romance subgenre that includes modern-day stories as opposed to historical stories.
"Contemporary" may be used to describe books that do not fall into other subgenres or may be combined with other subgenre indicators to more accurately describe a title, such as in the case of a contemporary romantic suspense or a contemporary paranormal romance.

Content Editor – editor whose main focus is your craft and story (as opposed to technical issues such as punctuation, which are the province of copy editors). Your editor will most likely edit both your content and copy, and you may also go through a copy editor and proofreader in later edit rounds.

Contest – competition. Numerous entities sponsor writing contests, some of which are extremely prestigious and can help you catch the attention of an editor or agent. Be careful, however, to enter only those contests conducted by reputable organizations. Small fees are often associated with entry and this is acceptable.

Continuing Conflict – conflict that carries through two or more books in a series.

Continuity – the degree to which details agree throughout your story. For example, if a character's eyes are green in chapter one, they should be green in chapter ten as well. Further, if a character walks away from another, they cannot suddenly kiss unless one of them approaches the other again.

Contract – binding agreement, usually written, that spells out the legal obligations of all contracted parties, as well as the terms under which a joint venture or project will be conducted.

Contract Terms – individual specifications within a contract, such as which legal jurisdiction will adjudicate disputes, when payments must be made, etc.

Copy Editor – editor whose main area of responsibility is within the technical realm: sentence structure, word choice, tense agreement, punctuation, etc.

Copyright – protected ownership of a document or other work that is ensured by obtaining a copyright from the government. Once a document is copyrighted, it cannot be copied or excerpted without your permission, except in special cases such as parody and derivative work (like fan fiction). In some cases, your publisher will take out a copyright on your book; in other cases, copyright is left up to the author.

Cover Art – art on the front of your book. For print books, this generally refers to the front, back and spine art. Cover art is extremely important because so many people choose books based on the cover. You will probably have input into the development of your cover art, and small presses sometimes allow authors to provide their own art, but the publisher has final say in all cover art decisions. When self-publishing, you are responsible for obtaining appropriate cover art.

Cover Artist – person responsible for creating cover art. This may be a staff or freelance position.

Cover Price – price of the book, so named because, for print books, the price usually appears on the cover.

Cover Slick – high quality print out of your cover art usually printed on glossy paper. Cover slicks are used in physical press and marketing kits and authors of e-books might also use them in place of print books at book signings.

Craft – the portion of writing that has to do with the techniques and methodologies of storytelling. This includes characterization, show don't tell, scene/summary, etc. Many writing workshops focus on craft because it is such a significant—and sometimes complex—part of writing.

Credit – often listed in the acknowledgements section, a credit gives you an opportunity to thank someone who helped you write or research your book. (See also acknowledgement.)

Credit with Apology – acknowledgement in which you assume responsibility in advance for any errors involving the information a research source provided. This helps protect the reputation of professionals such as doctors and forensic technicians in case you make a mistake.

E.g.: Many thanks to Dr. Jessica Jackson for invaluable information about bat physiology. Any and all mistakes are mine alone.

Crit Group – see critique group.

Critique – critical evaluation of your manuscript (or a part of it), intended to help you emphasize the good and correct the problematic. There are as many ways to critique as there are writers. Some write up formal critiques, others use the track changes function in the document to make comments, others provide verbal feedback, and others use some combination of methods. Published authors often offer critiques as raffle prizes.

Critique Group – group of writers who critique each other's work and encourage one another on the publication journey. (See also critique partner.)

Critique Partner – individual who critiques your work, provides encouragement, etc. Your critique partner is usually the first person to read your manuscript. You may have more than one, but choose carefully. Your critique partner needs to be willing to invest in you, be honest with you, and tell you things you don't want to hear—and you owe him or her the same.

Crit Partner – see critique partner.

Cross-genre – book that crosses or combines two or more genres, such as a fantasy mystery or paranormal romance.

Customer Review – book review written by a reader rather than a professional reviewer. The web contains several independent reader review sites and most online booksellers allow customers to leave reviews.

CWD – stands for "chicks with dicks." Slang way of saying that the males in a book speak and act like women rather than like men.

D

D&A – see delivery and acceptance.

Daily Pages – self-assigned writing quota, measured in terms of pages. Setting a daily goal often helps writers stay motivated and on-task.

Daily Words – self-assigned writing quota, measured in terms of word count. Setting a daily goal often helps writers stay motivated and on-task.

Dark Moment – moment at which it seems all is lost. In romance, this is when it appears the couple cannot possibly make the relationship work. Of course, in romance, the author always manages to resolve the dark moment to create an HEA or HFN.

Dash – the mark separating words and definitions in this book. (-) Note that a dash (not an ellipse) is used to set off a phrase or to indicate that a speaker is being cut off mid-word or mid-sentence. Ellipses (…) are used to indicate trailing off. (See also em dash, double dash, ellipse)

E.g.: Danny wondered—not for the first time—what Grandpa thought about the matter.

Note: if you replace with ellipses (Danny wondered…not for the first time…what   Grandpa thought about the matter), Danny just sounds, well, slow.

Deadline – time or date by which something is due. This could be an initial manuscript, a round of edits, or a decision about a contract.

Debut Novel – an author's very first published novel.

Dedication – text at the beginning of a book, prior to the story, in which the author dedicates the book to one or more people. This is somewhat different than an acknowledgement.

Deep POV – when the author provides exceptionally clear and effective insight into a character's inner feelings, thoughts, and emotions. Some use the term only to refer to such depth in third-person POV while others apply it to any point of view.

Delivery – point at which the author delivers something, such as a round of edits or a manuscript. When a book is accepted on proposal, this usually refers to the point at which the actual manuscript is delivered. For full-length submissions, delivery most often means completion of a print-ready manuscript with all edits completed.

Delivery and Acceptance – point at which a book—usually one accepted on proposal—has been delivered and is accepted by the publisher.

Delivery Date – deadline by which a manuscript or round of edits are due. This is often specified in your contract. You may incur penalties if you miss your delivery date without prior notice, and you will certainly irritate your agent and publisher—particularly if it becomes a pattern.

Dependent Clause – group of words that don't form a complete sentence, but still contain a subject and a verb. Stacking too many dependent clauses within a sentence can lead to bulky sentences and, in some cases, confusion. On occasion, however, you can actually do this on purpose to create the impression that your character is confused or frazzled. The following example contains a whopping six dependent clauses.

> E.g.: <u>When Max found the letter</u>, he didn't tell Sabrina <u>because he wasn't sure how she would take it</u> <u>and he didn't want her to be upset</u>, <u>especially since she was about to leave for the funeral</u> <u>and he wasn't sure if the letter's claims were true anyway</u> <u>or if he even cared</u>.

Dialog – text in which a character is speaking aloud. Many new authors struggle with punctuating dialog. The terminal punctuation mark in the last sentence of dialog (usually a period, comma, exclamation point, or question mark) goes inside the end quote mark. If the last sentence of dialog would normally end with a period, and it is followed by a dialog tag, use a comma instead.

E.g.: "You've lost your ever-loving mind," Sarah said.

Dialog Confusion – point in the dialog at which a reader cannot tell which character is speaking. This can usually be solved by a judiciously placed dialog tag, thought tag, or action tag.

Dialog Tag – text immediately before or after a line of dialog that indicates the speaker, either through use of a name or pronoun. The most common verb in a dialog tag is "said," but you may also use other verbs, such as "whispered" or "shouted." See also thought tag and action tag.

E.g.: "That's absurd," she said.

Digital Presence – term used to describe an author or publisher that has published e-books.

Digital Edition – electronic version of a book.

Digital-first – publishing model in which the electronic version of the book comes out first and the print version releases later—if at all. Can be a descriptor: "digital-first publisher" or "digital-first publishing."

Digital List Price – regular list price of an e-book, before any sales or discounts.

Digital Press – house that publishes e-books, either exclusively or predominantly.

Digital Publishing – the publication of e-books.

Digital Rights Management – technology that limits the use of digital content such as e-books. This includes library or device-to-device loaning software that causes access to the file to expire at a pre-set time.

Direct Selling – model in which an author sells books, either in person or on a website, directly to the consumer rather than through the publisher or a bookseller. Some contracts explicitly forbid direct selling; others allow it. Self-published authors often direct sell when they give speeches or presentations or participate in book fairs or signings.

Discount Price – refers to the discounted price at which booksellers and other retailers purchase your book from the publisher. Discounts allow the bookseller to make a profit. Your royalties may be based on the discount price rather than the list price when sold through a retail outlet.

Double-spaced – formatting tool that inserts a blank line between lines of text. Virtually every publisher and agent requires submissions to be double-spaced.

Dystopia – antonym of "utopia." A dystopia is a world, community, or society that is extremely bad or frightening. Examples include worlds in which all aspects of life are controlled by the state or by a supremely powerful private entity.

DLP – stands for digital list price.

Domestic Sales – sales of your book within your home country.

Double Dash – two dashes in a row, used to set off a section of text from the surrounding sentence. Some publishers prefer double dashes while others prefer the em dash.

Draft – early version of your manuscript that generally needs additional revision before you submit it to a publisher.

DRM – stands for digital rights management.

DubCon – short for dubious consent.

Dubious Consent – scene(s) in which the heroine's consent to a sexual act is in question. She may resist, either physically or verbally. With the exception of erotica—and very occasionally in erotic romance—you need to make it clear that the heroine has changed her mind and wants to have sex before any penetration occurs or you risk alienating readers (assuming your editor doesn't make you change it). Dubious content can be extremely controversial.

Dump – term used for a first draft in which you simply get all your ideas out of your head and onto the page. Dumps generally require extensive revision. Pantsers almost always dump; plotters not as often.

Earn Out – when your royalties based on actual sales equal or exceed the amount of your advance. Earning out – preferably quickly – is good for you, partly because it means you are making money and partly because it will increase publisher confidence in your future books.

E-book – short for electronic book and the more commonly-used term.

Echo Words – incidences of the same word used more than once in close proximity. This includes forms of the same word, such as "hear" and "heard." Most of the time, you should change one or more of the incidences to another word, but you may occasionally use echo words to make a point.

> E.g.: The spring sun beat down, <u>warming</u> the pavement below our bare feet. "It sure is <u>warm</u> out," Sally said.

Editor – professional tasked with helping you revise your manuscript into the best possible story. Editors come in several varieties, each with his or her own specialty.

Editor/Agent Appointment – short, scheduled appointment, usually during a conference or other event, during which you may pitch your book to an editor or agent.

Editor/Agent Pitch – pitch given during an editor/agent appointment.

Editorial Letter – letter outlining the revisions you are expected to make before your book can be published.

Editorial Revisions – revisions assigned, suggested, or made by your editor after your book has been accepted (as opposed to those you complete on your own prior to submission). These may include technical, craft, and/or story revisions.

Edit Round – period during which your editor sends you revisions and you complete them and return the new draft. You may go through several edit rounds before your book is ready for publication.

Electronic Book – digital version of your book. Often shortened to "e-book." In most cases, e-books are available in a variety of file formats.

Electronic Publishing – see digital publishing.

Electronic Rights – rights to the electronic version of your book. These may or may not be contracted separately from print rights and usually involve a different royalty percentage.

Electronic Small Press – term used to describe digital-first publishers who publish and sell a relatively small number of books annually. No specific threshold separates small presses from large presses.

Electronic Submission – submission method in which an electronic file is e-mailed or dropboxed to an editor or agent as opposed to being sent through the mail in hard copy format. Most submissions are electronic these days and many publishers no longer accept hard copy submissions.

Ellipse – those are those three periods in a row. (…) Note that an ellipse indicates someone is trailing off. Use dashes (or em dashes or double dashes, depending on your publisher's preference) to set off a phrase or to indicate that a speaker is being cut off mid-word or mid-sentence." (See also dash)

> E.g.: "Gloria, I don't know how to say this…" (speaker trails off)
>
> as opposed to:
>
> "Gloria, I don't know how to say this—"

"Just say it, Donald!" (Gloria cuts Donald off with her line.)

Em Dash – dash that has the same width as a capital "M" in the same font. Some house style guides use the em dash in place of a double dash. The em dash differs from the en dash in that the em is wider and does not have spaces on either side.

> Eg: An em dash—looks like that, but an en dash – looks like that.

Emotionally Satisfying Ending – the "feel good" ending characteristic of romance novels. The reader feels that conflict has been fully overcome, that the romantic relationship will thrive, and, most importantly, that they enjoyed reading the story.

En Dash – dash that has the same width as a capital "N" in the same font. Some house style guides use the en dash in place of a double dash. The en dash differs from the em dash in that the em is wider and does not have spaces on either side.

> Eg: An em dash—looks like that, but an en dash – looks like that.

Entry Requirements – stipulations regarding who may enter a contest and how and when submissions must be received. Virtually all contests spell out their entry requirements and most will disqualify you for failing to follow them, so read carefully and ask questions first.

Epilogue – short bit of text placed after the last chapter that is usually used to tie up loose ends or show an event in the future.

E-pub – short for e-publisher or e-published (generally "e-pubbed"). EPUB is also an electronic file format.

ER – stands for erotic romance.

E-reader – hand-held electronic device on which the primary functions is reading e-books and other electronic files. Some e-readers may have advanced functionality that qualifies them as a tablet.

EroRom – short for erotic romance.

Erotica – genre in which the main character's sexual journey is the primary focus. Language is frank and explicit; sex is prolific. Erotica may or may not include a love story (as opposed to erotic romance, in which a love story with HFN or HEA is primary and required). Most consider erotica to be a separate genre, distinct from all subgenres of romance.

Erotic Romance – subgenre of romance that features frequent sex written in frank language. May include kink, but need not, and must feature an HFN or HEA.

ESP – stands for electronic small press.

Established Author – author who has had one or more successful published works. Such authors have usually built a readership and platform and therefore represent less risk to publishers, agents, and booksellers than does a debut author.

Excerpt – portion of a book or other work that is made available without a purchase commitment. For example, online booksellers may offer an excerpt so that potential buyers can see if the writer's style interests them. You may also use excerpts to promote your book, though your contract will most likely restrict the total percentage of the book that can be accessed free.

Exclusive Rights - rights which are held solely by one person or entity. For example, an overseas distributor might have the exclusive right to distribute your book in its country or region.

Exposition – portions of your book that provide history, back story, or other information directly rather than in dialog or through action scenes. Some exposition is necessary and useful, but excessive exposition creates an info dump and should be avoided.

External Conflict – conflict that originates outside the character or couple, such as another person, a situation, distance, a natural disaster, etc. See also internal conflict. Both types of conflict are generally present in a good story.

Fair Use – portion of intellectual property law that outlines when and how copyrighted material may be quoted directly. Criticism and parody are the most commonly protected uses, though limited educational use is also permitted.

Fandom – the community of fans surrounding a given topic, television show, book, movie, character, series, etc.

FanFic – see fan fiction.

Fan Fiction – works of fiction, often short, that are based on characters and/or worlds already developed in another book, comic book, graphic novel, television show, movie, etc.

Fantasy – fiction to which magic, imaginary worlds, supernatural beings, and similar elements are integral. Fantasy generally avoids the scientific theory and elements common in science fiction and is distinguished from paranormal in that paranormal books are usually set in our world while fantasy is usually set in a fictional world. Subgenres include heroic, epic, low fantasy, and superhero.

Fiction – works that are not true stories. (See also non-fiction.)

File Format –the encoding specific to various software programs. You can tell the format from the file extension and not all devices can read all file types.

Film Rights – rights to turn your book into a movie or television show. Film rights may be sold separately from other rights.

Filtering – creating an extra layer of perception within a character's point of view by saying the character felt or noticed something rather than simply having the action occur. This places distance between the reader and the character, pulling the reader slightly out of the story, and is usually undesirable.

> E.g.: She felt the warmth of his hands on his shoulders. (The unfiltered version might be "His hands were warm on her shoulders.")

First – generally stands for first-person point of view.

First Draft – first version of your book, before edits or corrections. Don't plan for this to be publishable.

First Look – contract clause that grants an agent or publisher the first opportunity to make an offer on your next book. The clause may be restricted to the next work of a certain length or within a specific genre or subgenre. Distinct from a right of first refusal.

First Person – refers to first person point of view. In first person, you are writing directly from the character's viewpoint as though he or she is actually speaking. You (and the reader) can see and feel only what the character sees and feels. Some readers, editor, and houses are not fond of first person as they feel it limits the story. Others have no such concerns.

> E.g.: I walked toward the fountain, wondering if I could possibly be seeing my brother again.

First Three – refers to the first three chapters of your book. When an editor or agent asks for a partial, they usually want the first three or the first three and last. This is why it's so important to have a good hook at the end of the third chapter.

Flashback – point at which the story steps into a past moment or scene, often via a character's memory, and usually in a time prior to when your story actually begins.

Flash Fiction – extremely short fiction, usually under 1,000 words. The goal of flash fiction is to provide a complete, satisfying story in a "flash." Often used as a clean writing exercise, flash fiction teaches you to choose words carefully, make every sentence count, and avoid bloat.

Flow – the way in which your sentences, paragraphs and scenes lead smoothly into those following.

Forced Seduction – a scene in which the hero forces himself upon the heroine regardless of her feelings. He can usually get away with this either because he is in a position of power over the woman (such as a visiting nobleman and a parlor maid) or because the woman is only making a show of resisting the seduction. Some contend that forced seduction is essentially rape, while others assert that the difference exists in the hidden or partially obscured inner desires of the heroine.

Foreign Rights – rights to print or distribute your book in locations outside your home country. Foreign rights may be contracted by geography.

Foreign Sales – sales of your book outside your home country.

Foreshadowing – an event, action, or line of dialog that hints at a secret yet to be unveiled.

Formatting – preparing your book for submission, upload, or print in terms of spacing, margins, hard returns, indents, etc.

Fourth Wall – see breaking the third (or fourth) wall.

Fractured Fairy Tale – story that modifies a classic fairy tale in some unexpected or unique way.

Freelance – self-employed on a project basis rather than a direct or contract employee of a specific company. If you self-publish, you will need to consider freelancers such as cover artists and editors.

Free Read – scene, short story, or other work offered to readers free of charge. Such reads may be posted on blog or other sites or may be self-published by the author. Some publishers also contract with authors to provide free reads, often at a flat rate or a graduated rate based on sales. Only those works that are always free (as opposed to those offered free for a limited time) are generally classified as free reads.

Friends to Lovers – romance trope in which long-time friends become romantically involved.

Front List – newly published books, often those published less than one year prior. Sometimes spelled as one word: "frontlist"

Full – short for a full manuscript. (See also partial).

Futuristic – work that takes place in the distant (or at least fairly distant) future. It usually reflects a version of our own world that is much changed from modern day.

Galleys – short for galley proofs. Preliminary versions of a book prepared for publication. These are generally used so that all parties can review the final layout for issues and errors. They may also be used as ARCs. Galleys may be printed or electronic and paper galleys often have wide margins for making notes.

Genre Conventions – "rules" or standards inherent to a particular genre or subgenre. For example, romance novels must have a HFN or HEA ending. In category romance, the hero should show up within the first few (some say first two) pages of the book. Most genres and subgenres have a set of standard conventions, though some are less set in stone than others.

Genre Fiction – works of fiction that clearly fit within a certain genre, such as romance, mystery, thriller, science fiction, etc. Contrasts with mainstream fiction and literary fiction.

Genre First Look – contract clause granting the publisher an opportunity to be the first house to consider and offer a contract on the next book the author writes within the same subgenre. Such clauses usually provide the publisher a set number of days to review the manuscript and offer a contract before the author can submit his or her work to another house.

Ghost Writer – person who does the actual writing of a story, usually for a celebrity or for a well-known writer who has difficulty crafting certain types of scenes. Ghost writers are not credited and most sign confidentiality agreements that prevent them from disclosing their involvement in the project. May be spelled as one word: "ghostwriter."

Giveaways – stuff you give away for free. Giveaways can range from copies of your book to gift cards and prizes, to promotional items such as pens and pins.

GMC – stands for "goal, motivation, conflict."

Goal – the thing your main character wants most. In romance, this usually involves some aspect of a successful relationship.

Golden Heart – annual writing contest for unpublished authors, sponsored by Romance Writers of America.

Goodie Bag – bag (not always in the literal sense of the word "bag"), you receive at a conference or other event, containing freebies from writers, publishers, and others.

Goodie Room – room in which conference attendees can pick up giveaways donated by authors, publishers, and others. Goodies range from bookmarks to pens to books and everything in between.

Goodreads – one of the largest reader review sites currently in operation.

Grammar – refers to the set of rules that creates the structure of language: tenses, verb-noun agreement, syntax, etc.

Grant of Rights – action in which one party grants another the right to do something. For example, when you sign a publishing contract, you grant the publisher the right to publish your book.

Hachette – one of the Big Six New York publishers.

Happily Ever After – term used to describe an ending in which the hero and heroine (or other primary pairing) commit to one another on a permanent basis, usually via a promise of marriage or similar commitment. Frequently abbreviated to HEA, this is the required ending for most subgenres of romance. Happily Ever After is distinct from Happy for Now, in which the pairing commits to one another on a trial basis.

Happy for Now – ending in which the hero and heroine (or other primary pairing) commit to one another for the time being. Often abbreviated HFN, this is an alternate to HEA, in which the couple commits on a theoretically permanent basis, such as an engagement or marriage.

Hard Copy – physical copy of something, such as a document. This includes not only bound books and printouts of manuscripts, but also documents coded onto hard data devices such as DVDs.

Hard Copy Submission – submission process that requires you to submit a hard copy of your manuscript. Once the only possible submission method, hard copy submissions are now fairly rare.

Hardcover – version of a print book with rigid covers (as opposed to paperbacks, which are softcover). Also called "hardback."

Harlequin – arguably the largest and best-known category romance house.

HarperCollins – one of the Big Six New York publishers.

HEA – see Happily Ever After

Head-hopping – changing POV frequently and without notice while in third-person point of view or showing one character's thoughts while in a different character's point of view. Head-hopping should be eliminated as it confuses both the story and the reader.

Heat Levels – classification that reflects the amount of sex and sexual tension in a romance novel. The lowest level (sweet) indicates kissing/hugging/hand-holding only. The highest levels are usually reserved for kink and ménage (usually found in erotic romance).

Heat Rating – rating system used by some publishers or review sites to indicate the amount of sex and sexual tension in a romance novel. Ratings may be represented by numbers, chili peppers, flames, or any of a number of other "hot" images.

Hero - main male character.

Heroine – main female character.

Het – stands for heterosexual and used to indicate stories in when the primary pairing consists of one male and one female.

HFN – see Happy for Now.

High Discount Sales – book sales in which the discount price is significantly lower than the list price. This generally means lower royalties per book sold, but the trade-off is often a higher volume of sales.

Historical – story set in a historical period and a perennial favorite romance subgenre. Popular eras include Regency, Victorian, Civil War, and Medieval as well as early American western. Historical set in the last 50 years or so may be called "modern historical."

Hook – story feature or event that generates interest. Used generally, this can mean any action throughout the book that keeps readers engaged. Often, however, the term is used to mean a hook line, a line that sums up the essence of your story and makes readers want to buy the book.

Horror – scary books. Horror novels often contain some sort of paranormal element and tend to have higher body counts and more extreme gore levels than thrillers or mysteries. Subgenres include creepy kids, psychological, and gothic.

House – short for publishing house.

House Style – set of spelling, grammar, and punctuation rules used by your publishing house. In fiction, this is often a modified version of CMOS paired with a preferred dictionary for spelling, but each house has its own style. The house style is non-negotiable. If your house says "website" should be written as "Web site," the published version will read "Web site."

House Style Guide – document that details the house style.

I

Imprint – subsidiary brand within a publishing house. Imprints generally have a specific mission and may publish only one type of book or one genre or subgenre. Small publishers often do not have imprints, but large publishers can have anywhere from a few to more than 50 imprints.

Inciting Incident – see inciting moment.

Inciting Moment – moment at which something happens to begin the real action of the story. In romance, this is almost always when the hero and heroine (or other pairing) meet.

Indemnity – protection, usually against legal action or financial loss. Many contracts require the author to indemnify the agent or publisher against legal action resulting from author actions such as failing to get permission to quote copyrighted works.

Indie – stands for independent, which essentially means self-published. An "indie book" is one that is self-published; and "indie author" is one who self-publishes.

Some use this term to refer to digital-first and small presses as well.

Info Dump – section of text in which the author exposes a tremendous amount of information, often character backstory, all at one time rather than doling it out throughout the book or exposing the information through action or dialog.

Inspirational Romance – romance novels with a faith-based theme, usually Christian. These books contain the common romance genre formula of overcoming conflict and falling in love, but emphasis is on developing the couple's relationship in light of their faith. Physical attraction may well play a role and kissing "on camera" is permitted, but sex occurs exclusively after marriage and, if present in the book at all, will be closed door. Sometimes called "inspy" (in' spee).

Inspy – see Inspirational Romance.

Internal Conflict – conflict that arises from within a character, such as trust issues, insecurity, or other personal baggage. (See also external conflict.)

Interracial Romance– romance in which the hero and heroine (or other members of the primary pairing) have different ethnic or racial origins. In theory, a true interracial romance explores the cultural differences and conflicts caused by the difference in ethnicity, but some publishers classify any book featuring an interracial couple as an interracial romance.

I/R – stands for interracial romance.

ISBN – stands for International Standard Book Number. Unique identifier assigned to books available for purchase. Different versions of the same book, including print and electronic versions, receive different numbers. Numbers are 10 or 13 digits, depending on when they were assigned. If you are self-publishing, you may have to purchase your own ISBN.

J

Junior Editor – editor with less experience and authority than a senior editor. Depending on the house, a junior editor might work with an author on early revisions before bringing in a senior editor in the final edit rounds.

Keyword – word or phrase people type into a search engine to find that they're looking for. For example, a reader might type "Regency romance novels" or "writing blogs." The search engine will scan all the available sites and look for the best matches. You can often create a list of keywords for your website or blog page. Note that search engines also scan the file names of any uploaded pictures, so be sure to rename your photos appropriately.

Kink – term used to describe "non-typical" sexual behaviors such as BDSM, ménage, fetishism, etc.

Kirkus Book Reviews – one of the largest, most well-known multi-genre review sites.

Layout – the way your book looks on the printed page. If your book is "in layout," the publisher is working to set up all the pages in preparation for print.

LGBT – stands for lesbian, gay, bisexual, transgender.

Librarian – professional who runs the library. Librarians can be great allies because readers often ask them for recommendations. On some review sites, a person authorized to add information about a book, or to classify it within the system, is also called a librarian.

Library – the place where books live and can be checked out by members. Yes, you probably know what a library is already, but you'll want to begin thinking about the role it plays in your sales and readership. This includes both brick-and-mortar libraries and also online lending libraries for e-books.

Light – less intense. This is usually followed by a genre, such as fantasy or erotic romance.

Like Party – event, usually held exclusively online, during which several authors get together and like each other's books on various review and online bookseller sites so as to increase the desirability of all the authors' books. Variations include liking one another's blogs or social media pages.

Limited Omniscient POV – see third-person limited.

Limited POV - see third-person limited.

Line – may have several meanings. It most often means a named set of subgenre books at a given publisher. For example, "Harlequin Intrigue" is the name of Harlequin's romantic suspense line, while its inspirational romance line is called "Love Inspired." "Line" may also refer to a line of dialog or a line of text on a page.

Line Editor – editor who specializes in line edits.

Line Edits – last round of edits (besides proofing) in which an editor goes through your book line by line to look for grammar, punctuation, and continuity errors, dialog confusion, echo words, etc.

Lines – usually refers to line edits.

List Price – price at which your book is listed for sale. Certain sales outlets might offer buyers a discount off the list price, either permanently or as a special promotion.

Literary Agent – see agent.

Literary Fiction – "serious" literature that is critically deemed to deal with universal and lasting themes and to have the potential to remain relevant and readable indefinitely. Fiction is generally broken into two categories: literary and popular or commercial (which includes almost all genre fiction).

Literary Scout – individual whose entire job is to look for books to acquire. Scouts generally work for foreign publishing houses or scouting agencies and are usually looking for books that are doing well in their home countries and for which the foreign rights are still available. Scouts may also work for film or television production companies, in which case they are looking for books that would do well if turned into movies or television programs.

Literature – written works, especially those that are considered groundbreaking, unusually well-written, or likely to remain relevant and appealing across time. There's still much debate, particularly in academic circles, about whether genre fiction can be literature.

Local Chapter – chapter of an organization, such as Romance Writers of America, that is based on geography. Like mine: Georgia Romance Writers.

Logline – short summary of a television show or movie that describes what it is and also provides the hook for potential viewers. This is similar to the blurb for a book, but is usually just a single sentence. Loglines are also used to pitch movie scripts in Hollywood. May be spelled as two words: log line.

Loose Ends – subplots or events that never get wrapped up and questions that never get answered. Readers hate them. Note that this is different from a continuing conflict in a series.

MacMillian – one of the Big Six publishers in New York.

Main Character – the central characters in your book. In a romance, this is usually the primary pairing.

Mainstream – refers to mainstream fiction, popular fiction (not literary fiction) that does not fall within a particular genre, but rather has mass appeal.

Major Conflict – substantial conflict that indicates a significant and problematic difference in goals, values, etc. This might include a killer conflicting with a detective in mystery or potential lovers with vastly differing ethics in romance. This is generally at the core of a story.

Manuscript – the text of a narrative work (as opposed to a screen or stageplay, which has a script.) "Manuscript" generally denotes a submitted work rather than a published one. Once it's published, it becomes a "book." Often abbreviated ms.

Marketing – activities, including advertising, price strategy, publicity, promotions, and more, that are intended to create interest in your book. Most publishing houses have a marketing department, but the amount of work the department puts into your book will depend on prior and anticipated success.

Marriage of Convenience – romance trope in which the hero and heroine become committed or married and then fall in love later. This trope is particularly popular in the historical subgenre and often appears as an arranged marriage.

Mass Market Paperback – slightly smaller, somewhat less expensive version of a trade paperback that is designed to be sold through mass retailers such as drug and convenience stores as opposed to booksellers.

MC – can either stand for "main character" or "motivation, conflict."

Member Price – discounted price paid by a book club member.

Memoir – work of creative non-fiction in which the author recalls a specific event, person, or other memory using fiction-like storytelling devices.

Ménage – romantic or sexual relationship between three or more people.

Middle Grades – refers to middle grade fiction, fiction intended for readers aged roughly eight to 12. The protagonist is usually of a similar age and faces the kinds of internal and external situations typical of middle-grade children.

Midlist Author – author who does not reach bestseller rank, but sells well enough to be considered viable.

Minor Conflict – small, almost incidental conflicts that can be used to show differences or challenge the hero or heroine. For example, a romance novel heroine might see the hero's love of a food she detests as one more indicator that they are too different to be together.

M/M – stands for male/male and describes books in which the primary pairing consists of two men.

Mobipocket – a specific brand of e-reader software.

Motif – repeated image, phrase, or other item that has significance in a story. Used discerningly, motifs can help create depth and help further your primary theme(s).

Motivation – emotion, need, or situation that is driving your character toward his or her goal. If the goal is what she most wants, the motivation is why she wants it.

MS – abbreviation for "manuscript." Usually lowercased: "ms."

MSRP – stands for manufacturer's suggested retail price. See list price.

Multi-Author Anthology – see anthology.

Multi-author Blog – blog authored by two or more people. Such blogs have the benefit of reducing each author's blogging requirements and allowing for collaborative promotion, but, as with any joint venture, involvement of multiple parties can create complexity and stress.

Multi-book Deal – contract that includes both the current book and a specified number of future books, which may or may not be part of a series. Variations of this term specify the number of books contracted: "two-book deal," "thee-book deal," etc.

Multicultural – books in which the meeting of cultures is a main focus. In romance, the hero and heroine (or other pairing) are generally from different cultures or ethnicities. See also interracial romance.

Multi-genre – see cross-genre.

Multiple Submissions – sending more than one book to the same editor or house at the same time. It may also mean sending one book to several editors at the same house at the same time. Most houses strongly discourage—or outright forbid—multiple submissions. New writers often confuse this term with simultaneous submissions.

Multi-published – author who has published two or more books.

Muse – term many authors use to describe their inner inspiration. Some even name their muses.

Mystery – books containing a mystery as the primary plot. The mystery genre contains dozens of subgenres including cozy, caper, hard-boiled, police procedural, locked room, etc. The key conventions in mystery are that the perpetrator must be discovered and justice must be served.

NaNoWriMo – National Novel Writing Month. Held each November, this is an online event in which people from around the world attempt to write 50,000 words (the approximate equivalent of a 175-page novel) in 30 days. Focus is on productivity over perfection. The website offers word count tracking, a buddy system, and more. Many libraries and bookstores host write-ins throughout the month as well.

Narrative – storytelling on the part of the author. Essentially this is your story.

Nationals – refers to the national writer's conference sponsored annually by Romance Writers of America (as opposed to local chapter conferences.)

Net Sales – sales after discounts and returns. Your royalties may be based on this number.

New Release – book that has just been made available for purchase.

New York – traditionally, New York is the place where publishing happens. "New York" is often used to refer to the Big Six publishers, all of whom are in New York.

Niche – specialty. In publishing, this usually refers either to books that appeal only to a specialty market or to publishers who publish only very specific types of books. Examples of niche books might include those focused on local history or an esoteric research subject. Niche publishers might restrict offerings to a single subgenre of popular fiction, academic publications, poetry, etc.

Nom de Plume – literally means "name of the pen." See pen name.

Non-delivery – term that describes failure to meet a delivery deadline. It may also mean an author's failure to adequately, in the publisher's view, edit a book. Non-delivery may be cause for contract cancellation and may trigger penalty fees.

Non-fiction – works, including books and articles, that are true. This includes reference books (like this one), textbooks, narrative non-fiction, and memoirs. Conventions and submission guidelines are typically much different for non-fiction than for fiction.

Novel – work of book-length fiction that tells a story. Some use the term specifically to describe works of mainstream fiction rather than genre fiction.

Novel with Strong Romantic Elements – novel that does not follow all the conventions of a romance, but has many aspects of romance, such as a love story, romantic conflict and, often, an HFN or HEA.

Novelette – less commonly-used version of novella.

Novella – work that is somewhere between a short story and a full-length novel. Different publishers define novellas differently, with the lowest word counts beginning around 7,000 and the highest word counts beginning around 30,000. Some classify works between about 25,000 and 50,000 words as short novels. Novellas are usually only available as e-books, unless several are grouped into an anthology for print.

Novel-length Fiction – see book-length fiction.

NYT – stands for New York Times and generally refers to the New York Times bestseller list.

NYT Bestseller List – weekly list of bestselling novels— based on chain, independent, and online booksellers as well as mass retailers—that is published by the New York Times.

Objective POV – see third-person objective.

Off Screen – film term used to describe action that is not filmed, but merely referenced. The stageplay equivalent is off stage. Either might be used to describe action that is referenced, but not included, in a book's narrative.

Omniscient POV – see third-person omniscient.

On Acceptance – see upon acceptance.

On Delivery – see upon delivery.

Online Bookseller – bookseller whose operations are conducted completely online or the division of a brick-and-mortar store that is online.

Online Workshop – workshop conducted completely online. Many organizations offer such workshops on a variety of topics.

On Publication – see upon publication.

On Screen – opposite of off screen.

OOP – see out of print.

Open Door – action, usually sexual, that occurs on the page rather than simply being referred to later.

Option Clause – clause that gives a publisher or agent the option to do something in the future. Usually, the "something" is acquiring your next work.

Out Clause – any clause that gives you or your publisher the right to leave the agreement under certain circumstances, such as an inability to reach agreement on edits in a timely manner. Out clauses may include penalties for one or both parties.

Out of Print – no longer available for purchase new. Even though digital books are not printed, this term has come to apply to any book that is no longer available as a new print copy or a download from an online retailer.

Oxford Comma – comma that appears between the next-to-last and last items in a list. Possibly the most hotly debated item of punctuation in the professional writing world, use or non-use of the Oxford comma is dictated by the house style guide. Oxford comma supporters point out that its use or non-use can change the meaning of a sentence. Others contend that this situation is rare and that it is more efficient to use the Oxford comma as an exception when necessary rather than in every list. Also called a serial comma.

> E.g.: Joe had blue eyes, blond hair, and a well-muscled physique.

Pacing – the rate at which your story progresses. There is no one right pace. Thrillers are often quite fast-paced, with actions scenes coming right after one another—particularly near the end. Romantic comedies, however, need to allow time for the relationship to develop or they feel rushed. Also, your pace may vary throughout your book.

Pairing – two (or more, in some genres) characters who are linked, either romantically or in another way, such as in detective pairs.

PAN – stands for Published Author Network. This is an RWA classification that denotes publication paired with a minimum quantity of sales.

Pantser – term used to describe an author who prefers to write without a pre-planned plot or outline. Fans of this writing process feel it allows for greater freedom of character and story exploration, but admit that they must usually do far more rewriting than those who plan in advance (often called plotters).

Paranormal – books having to do with magic, the spirit world, or paranormal entities such as vampires and witches. Paranormal can be its own genre or can further modify another genre such as in paranormal romance or paranormal thriller.

Partial – portion of your manuscript, usually comprised of either the first three chapters or the first three plus the last. Editors and agents may request a partial before committing themselves to reading your entire novel. (See also full.)

Passive Voice – sentence structure in which the main noun (subject) is acted upon rather than acting independently.

> E.g.: <u>The door was kicked</u> shut by Pam.

Past Tense – writing about an event as though it has already happened. This is the preferred tense for most publishers, though some books are written in present tense.

> E.g.: She ran through the woods, screaming at the top of her lungs.

Pay-per-click – digital advertising type in which you pay when someone clicks on your ad.

Penguin – short for Penguin Group, one of the Big Six New York publishers.

Pen Name – name, other than his or her own, under which an author publishes books. Pen names are common, particularly for authors who write in more than one genre.

Permissions – grants of permission to do something. In publishing, this usually means something like quoting, excerpting, or distributing your book. On a web, blog, or social media site, you'll grant permissions such as who can post to your social media account or edit information in your blog.

Pirating – printing, quoting, excerpting, giving away or selling your book without permission. This is illegal. You, your publisher, and/or your attorney can send a cease and desist, though the pirate may not comply and you may have to take legal action to stop the activity.

Pirate Site – site that sells or gives away books for which it has not been granted permission.

Pitch – short speech or letter used to interest an editor or publisher in your book.

Pitch Appointment – appointment, usually at a conference or in an online forum, to pitch your book to an editor or agent, either in person or online.

Pitch Workshop – workshop, often at a conference or other event, focused specifically on helping you create or refine your pitch.

Platform – this is the virtual stage on which you stand so the world can see you. Your platform is built from your author brand, your readership, your social media presence, your organization memberships, your website, and anything else you do to be visible to readers. Publishers will expect you to build a platform and having one started before you submit can help your chances of being published—as long as your book is good!

Playwright – author of a stage or screen play.

Plot – the collective events, in sequence, which form the framework of your book. Plot is one of the most important elements of writing.

Plot Bunny – slang for a new story idea, usually one that appears at an inconvenient time, such as while you're trying to finish your current WIP. You may have to take time to write the idea down somewhere in order to clear it from your mind.

Plot Holes – gaps in your plot that keep the story from flowing smoothly. This could be a place where a character acts against his nature without any explanation, either at the time or in the future. It could also be a spot where you leave out information critical to future events or insert a random scene that has no relevance to the rest of the book. Plot holes are confusing, so close them up. Sometimes written as one word: plotholes.

Plot Points – milestone moments or events within your overall plotline. This might include the moment a romantic couple meets or the discovery of a second body in a mystery, horror or thriller.

Plotter – term used to describe an author who prefers to create a plan or outline before beginning to write a book. Fans of this writing process feel it allows for greater structure and minimizes rewriting, but admit that they must sometimes stop to replan if the story takes an unexpected turn while they are writing. See also pantser.

Plus Novel – category romance classification that denotes an unusually long book.

POD – stands for print on demand.

Point of View – the perspective from which the narrative is written. Includes first person (I, me, my), second person (you, your), and various categories of third person (he, she, they).

Popular Fiction – fiction that is written with the intent of telling a story to an audience (preferably a large one). This represents the vast majority of fiction sold today and includes all genre fiction as well as mainstream fiction. The primary goal might be said to engage readers in the story. It contrasts with literary fiction, in which the primary goal is the act of telling of the story and sales and engagement are secondary.

POV – stands for point of view.

POV Break – physical indicator of a POV Shift. Many publishers use extra spaces or a centered design element (such as a swirl or a fleur-de-lis) in print works and some quantity of asterisks in digital works.

POV Shift – point at which the point of view changes from one character to another or from third-person to first-person (or vice versa).

Premise – central concept of your story. It's said that the most powerful words in the English language are "what if." Your premise comes from a "what if?" What if two strangers were snowed in at a country estate with no outside contact?

What if a woman woke up on her 30th birthday to find out she's a witch?

Preorder – order that occurs before a book is available for physical or digital purchase. Both online and brick-and-mortar booksellers sometimes use preorder to create—or respond to—advance interest in a book.

Preorder Link – active url link that takes readers to the place they can preorder your book. You might include this on your website, blog, or social media sites.

Present Tense – writing about an event as though it is happening now.

> E.g.: She runs through the woods, screaming at the top of her lungs.

Press Release – print or electronic notification that is sent to members of the press to inform them of an upcoming, current, or past event. You might send a press release to your local newspaper or radio station to advise them of a new release or a book signing. The idea is to generate press coverage that will increase your visibility and, hopefully, your sales.

Print on Demand – type of publishing in which books are printed and bound as orders are placed rather than in advance. This is the opposite of traditional printing, which utilizes a print run model. Print on demand is used by most self-published authors as well as many digital and small presses because it reduces (or eliminates) the costs and storage requirements associated with printing up front and carrying inventory.

Print Rights – the right to publish the print version of your book. This may be broken down into segments, such as hardcover, mass market paperback, etc.

Print to Order – see print on demand.

Print Run – set quantity of books printed at one time for later distribution. This is the traditional method of print publishing.

PRO – RWA designation that denotes an RWA member who has submitted at least one completed manuscript to a royalty-paying publisher, regardless of acceptance.

Process – see writing process.

Prologue – sort of mini-chapter appearing prior to chapter one. Prologues are usually used to reveal a scene that occurs before the book begins (often many years earlier).

Promotion Clause – contract clause that requires the author to promote his or her books. Some may stipulate specific activities, such as maintenance of a website, and not all contracts contain such a clause.

Promotions – the activity associated with promoting a book, series, or author. Promotion is part of marketing, but tends to involve activities such as participating in book signings and handing out giveaways rather than traditional marketing such as press releases and paid advertising.

Proofing – see proofreading.

Proofreading – reading a book word by word to catch misspellings, extra spaces, punctuation mistakes, missing words, and other such errors. Most publishers use a proofreader as the final step before formatting and, if you self-publish, you should consider doing so as well.

Proposal – see book proposal.

Protagonist – main character, usually the "good guy." (See also antagonist.)

Pseudonym – see pen name.

Pubbed – short for "published." Used in words such as "unpubbed" and "e-pubbed."

Publication Date – date on which your book first becomes available for purchase.

Public Domain – refers to works that are not subject to copyright laws for one reason or another. These works are said to be owned by the public as a whole rather than any one individual.

Publicist – person whose professional specialty is generating publicity. Many houses have one or more on staff and, as an author, you can also hire a freelance publicist to work on publicizing you and your books.

Publicity – the activities surrounding generating press for your work or author brand. Publicity is part of marketing and includes writing press releases, giving interviews, etc. Note that all areas of marketing overlap to some extent, so what one person might consider "publicity" might be considered "promotions" by another.

Published Author Network – see PAN.

Publisher – entity responsible for actually producing your book in buyable format, be it e-book, hard copy, soft copy, audiobook, etc. Your editor will most likely work for your publisher, either as a direct employee or a freelancer, as will the marketing people, cover artist, proofreader, etc.

Publisher Contract – contract that stipulates how you and your publisher will interact. This can include clauses or sections on royalties, edits, deadlines, rights, etc.

Publisher's Weekly – electronic and print newsmagazine for the publishing industry. It includes announcements, reviews, new release information and more.

Publishing Agreement – see publisher contract.

Publishing House – the formal term for a publisher.

Punctuation – all the "marks" associated with writing sentences: periods, semicolons, ellipses, etc.

Purple Prose – excessively or unnecessarily fancy or ornate language, particularly when used to describe romantic or sexual encounters. Purple prose distracts the reader and is not a good thing.

PW – see publisher's weekly.

QR Code – short for Quick Response Code, this is the trademarked name of a specialized type of barcode. These are those pixelated little squares that you see on ads, cereal boxes, tradeshow booths, and just about anything else a marketer can think to stick one on. This type of code was originally developed for inventory and manufacturing purposes because it holds far more information than a typical barcode, but authors and publishers (and shoe companies, and real estate agents, etc.) most often use QR codes to direct a potential buyer with a smart phone to a specific website (such as your author website or a site where people can buy your book). Users can take a picture of the code with their phones and be taken directly to the website you have encoded.

Quoting – quoting directly from a published work, including a film, television show, website, song, or other non-print work. You may not do this without permission from the entity who owns the rights, unless the work is in the public domain.

Query – see query letter.

Query Letter – electronic or physical letter in which you briefly explain your book to an editor or agent in hopes that they will request a partial or full. There are entire books about to how to write a query letter. You should probably invest in one.

Raffle Basket – package donated for raffle at a conference or other event, usually to benefit a charitable effort. Such baskets, which need not be actual baskets and might be tote bags or any other type of container, can contain a wide variety of items including books and promo to foods and other items. They are often donated by authors, but may also be donated by publishers, cover artists, etc.

Random House – one of the Big Six New York publishers.

Reader – person who reads a book. Writers write because of readers. The success of your book depends on your readers. They will review, recommend, and promote a book and/or author they love, but the flipside is also true. Treat them right. Always.

Reader Review – book review completed by a reader who is not a professional reviewer, whether it be on a review site, online retailer site, blog, etc.

Readership – the collective term for all your readers. While each individual reader will be different, your readership might have some common characteristics in terms of sex, age, and other demographics. You might also find that they have similar preferences in terms of how they shop or choose books, which can help you identify good advertising markets.

Reading Fee – fee assessed by an editor, publisher, or other entity for reading your manuscript. With few exceptions, the industry agrees that you should not have to pay to have your book considered.

Read Time – can mean one of two things. The first is the time it takes an average reader to read your book. The second, and more common usage, refers to the time you should allow an editor or agent to read and respond to your manuscript before following up. In the latter case, the read time is often stated in the submission guidelines and may be called a response time.

Record of Submission – email or physical receipt showing when and how you submitted a full or partial manuscript to an editor or agent. You will want to keep track of when you submitted so that you know when to follow up and you may need to provide a record of submission for tasks such as applying for specialty memberships in certain national organization and providing backup documentation in a tax audit.

Redlines – collective term for all the editing marks and comments your editor applies to your manuscript. The term originates from the time when all communications were paper-based and editors would use a red pen so as to make their comments and marks stand out from the black type.

Regency – British historical period that technically occurred between 1811 and 1820, but is commonly extended to include the time period from about 1795 to 1837. Regency romances are those occurring in this time period and are considered a distinct sub-category of historical romance.

Reissue – to put a book back into distribution, either electronically or in print. Reissues may occasionally include bonus content such as a foreword by the author and may be issued by a different publisher or imprint (or even the author, after a reversion of rights).

Rejection – indication by an editor or agent that your submission is not right for them at this time. This might occur in person at a pitch, but most often happens via email or, occasionally, regular mail, as a rejection letter.

Rejection Letter – electronic or physical letter from an editor or agent stating that they are turning down your submission. Many such letters are either form letters or use standard—and usually brief—language. This is partly because editors and agents are very busy and partly because some authors react badly to specific criticism. If you get a rejection letter with specific praise or advice, treasure it and heed its message.

Rejection Slip – see rejection letter.

Remainders – print copies of books that are sold by a publisher at a deep discount in order to clear out inventory, usually because the book is no longer selling well enough to justify keeping the stock. Authors may receive reduced or no royalties for such books.

Request for Full – letter, email, or verbal conversation in which an editor or agent asks you to submit your full manuscript for consideration.

Request for Partial – letter, email, or verbal conversation in which an editor or agent asks you to submit a partial of your manuscript for consideration.

Rerelease – see reissue.

Reseller – any entity, online site, or brick-and-mortar store that sells your book, other than the publisher or wholesaler.

Reserves Against Returns – portion of your royalties held against projected returns. These funds are generally available for release after the period of time specified by your contract.

Response Time – time (number of days/weeks/months) that an editor or publisher needs to review your submission before you follow up. This varies drastically between entities and is often specified in the submission guidelines. If the specified response time passes, it is perfectly acceptable to send a polite (and brief) follow up requesting confirmation of receipt.

Retail Price – see list price.

Returns – copies of books returned to the publisher or wholesaler, usually due to low sales. You will not receive royalties for returns, unless they are eventually sold to another outlet.

Reversion of Rights – point at which the rights to a book revert to the author. This means that you can self-publish your book or offer it for reissue to another publisher. You can also revise it, change the ending, stick it in a drawer, or do almost anything else you want with it because it is once again your property. Note that, if the publisher created the cover art or other design, they retain rights to those elements. You may hear an author say she "got [her] writes back." This means the rights have reverted to the author.

Review – write-up of your book, often with a ranking attached. Reviews can be written by professional reviewers or by readers and may contain a description of your storyline and/or the reviewer's opinions about your book. Reviews can appear on review sites, in magazines, on blogs, at purchase sites, and in any number of other locations. You will get bad reviews; everyone does. You'll be happier if you accept this fact in advance.

Reviewer – person who reviews a book.

Review Site – website dedicated to reviews, in this case, of books.

Revise and Resubmit – special circumstance in which an editor or agent neither accepts nor rejects your manuscript, but instead invites you to make specific changes and resend the revised manuscript. Such requests require time and interest on the part of the editor or agent, so give them careful consideration. Even if you decide not to accept the offer, be sure to respond by thanking the editor or agent in a professional manner.

Revisions – essentially, changes made at the request of your editor or agent. These may occur before or after the book is accepted, but publication is generally contingent upon mutually-agreeable revisions. You will have to make revisions; everyone does. As with bad reviews, you will be happier if you accept this fact in advance.

Rewrites – see revisions.

Right of First Refusal – contract clause in which the publisher has the right to acquire your next work. It is often restricted to the next work in a series or in the same genre.

Rights – legal entitlements. In publishing, this usually means rights to print, sell, or distribute your book, or to do something else with it.

RITA – annual writing contest for published authors, sponsored by Romance Writers of America and named for its first president, Rita Clay Estrada.

Romance – fiction genre focused on a successful romantic relationship. The genre includes several subgenres, including romantic suspense, erotic, historical, contemporary, and paranormal. The term "romance" denotes a specific set of genre conventions, the most critical of which is a happy ending (often called an emotionally satisfying ending).

Romance Writers of America – largest and most well-known national organization of romance writers in the U.S. It is an incorporated, membership-based, non-profit organization that includes both local (geographic-based) and special interest chapters. It also hosts online workshops, an annual conference, and respected annual contests for both published and unpublished authors. Often abbreviated RWA.

Romantic Suspense – subgenre of romance fiction that includes elements of mystery or suspense. The romance is always primary, though the suspense aspect must be distinct. Romantic suspense novels may be single-title or category.

Romantic Thriller – subgenre of romance fiction that includes elements of a thriller. Edgier and grittier than romantic suspense, the crimes in a romantic thriller are usually more graphic, both in nature and in description, and the thriller aspect may be slightly more emphasized than the romance element.

Romantic Times – print magazine that includes reviews, articles, etc., and also maintains a large web presence with extended features. Often abbreviated RT, it hosts an annual reader/writer conference as well.

RomCon – generally refers to an annual reader/writer convention focused on the romance genre. However, there is also a website that includes reviews, blogs, and more.

Rough Draft – draft of your manuscript prior to any self–edits or other revisions.

Royalties – monies received by the author for each copy of a book sold. This is your income on your published books.

Royalty Percentage – percentage of a book's sales price that is paid to you as royalties. This will be specified in your contract and will vary based on the publisher, type of book, number of authors on the project, entity that actually sells the book, etc.

Royalty Period – set period for which royalties are counted, reported, and paid. For example, you might be paid by the calendar month for sales on your publisher's website, but quarterly for sales through other outlets. Additionally, the period for which you get a check may not be the month or quarter immediately prior because there is sometimes a processing delay (kind of like hourly paychecks, which are often distributed a week after the pay period).

Royalty Statement – electronic or paper statement that summarizes the amount of royalties you have received for a specific royalty period. Most break out different books, book types, and outlets so that you can see what's doing well where.

RT – see Romantic Times.

RT Booklovers Convention – annual reader and writer convention hosted by Romantic Times.

RT Book Reviews – section of Romantic Times dedicated to book reviews. Considered highly prestigious in the romance fiction community.

RTF – stands for rich text file. This type of file can be read by most word processing programs and is therefore one of the preferred file types for submissions.

Run-on Sentence – sentence that goes on and on with a lot of clauses and extra words and even, possibly, complete changes of subject, that can be very confusing to the reader and really ought to be divided into two sentences or possibly three, or maybe don't even say anything important at all and should be cut. Like that one.

RWA – see Romance Writers of America.

RWR – stands for Romance Writers Review, the monthly magazine sent to members of Romance Writers of America.

S

Said Alternative– verb used in place of "said" in a dialog tag; intended to convey action or state of mind. Okay, so this isn't a real term. But it is a real—and important—concept. Many industry professionals feel that said alternatives should be used sparingly so as to avoid author interference and recommend the use of action tags or thought tags instead.

E.g.: "Don't leave me," she sobbed.

Sales – can refer to the number of your books sold and/or the dollars generated by those books.

Sales Channels – outlets through which your books are sold. This can include online retailers and booksellers, brick-and mortar booksellers, mass market retailers, etc. Royalties and terms may vary by channel.

Sales Rank – rank maintained by Amazon and some other sites. This indicates where your book ranks, in terms of number of copies sold, compared to all available books. Some sites break ranking down further, ranking book sales by genre and subgenre.

Sans Serif – font in which the letters do not have serifs (the small bars or hooks at the ends of letter strokes).

Scene – section of the book in which something important happens to move the story forward. For example, perhaps the "coffee shop scene" is where the hero and heroine meet or where the police find a clue to the killer.

Scene Break – indicator that the scene has changed within a chapter. Different publishers use different characters to indicate scene break. Three asterisks is a commonly-used indicator, at least in draft form.

Scene/Summary – craft term that refers to knowing which information is important enough to deserve a scene and which should be "summarized" in connecting text.

Science Fiction – genre that incorporates science-based theory as a significant portion of the plot. This often includes astronomical theory such as space travel, wormholes, and alien life, but can also biological and chemical experimentation and more.

Screenplay – script for a screen production, most often a movie. Screenwriting varies somewhat from novel writing, as it is told predominantly through dialog.

Screenwriter – person who writes a screenplay.

Script – the "book" or printed dialog and direction for a screenplay, television show, or stage play.

Search Engine – Internet program that helps users find sites and data. This includes the ability for readers to find your book. (See also search engine optimization.)

Second Person – point of view in which the author is speaking directly to the reader. While this is common in how-to and self-improvement books, it's rare to find an entire work of fiction told in second person. On occasion, however, a book, or stage- or screenplay might contain a short segment in second person. This is known as breaking the third (or fourth) wall.

Secondary Character – term for all the characters in your book other than the main characters. Think of the supporting cast in a movie. Secondary characters are important because they help build your main characters' world and can be used to reveal or hide information, to provide comic relief, and more. They may also become the foundation for one or more sequels.

Secret Baby – one of the oldest and most common of the romance tropes. The couple breaks up for one reason or another without the hero knowing the heroine is pregnant. The plot of books featuring this trope generally revolve around the hero finding out (often many years later) about the child and on how the couple resolves their issues— including the lack of trust engendered by the secret—and reach a happy ending.

Seeking Representation – actively looking for an agent.

Self-edits – edits initiated by you, the author, as opposed to those suggested by your agent or editor. This usually happens prior to submission.

Self-pubbed – short for self-published.

Self-published – author-published work, usually facilitated through a digital and/or POD publishing service. Not the same as vanity publishing.

Sell-in – the number of books that are shipped to various retailers to be sold. See also sell-through.

Sell-through – the number of shipped books that actually sell.

Senior Editor – editor with extensive experience. Senior editors can often make final decisions on books and editing disputes.

Sense of Place – the concept of creating a feeling or vision in the reader's mind about where your story takes place. For example, you might talk about rush hour traffic and crowds on the sidewalk to show a big city or incorporate regional dialects or accents to establish sense of place.

Sentence Structure – the way in which a sentence is arranged. Sentence structure can be used to accomplish many goals including showing a character's voice or state of mind or increasing or decreasing a scene's pace.

SEO – stands for search engine optimization. This is the process of making your website, book titles, and/or author name come up near the top of the results list in searches.

Serial – story told in individual increments or installments. Different from a series, in which each book is separate story with overlapping elements.

Serial Comma – see Oxford comma.

Series – generally refers to a set of books that have common characters and may continue an overarching storyline. May also refer to series romance.

Series First Look – contract clause in which the publisher has the right to make an offer on your next book in a series.

Series Romance – see category romance.

Serif Font – font in which the letters have serifs (the small bars or hooks at the ends of letter strokes).

Setting – world, locale, or area in which your story is set. This could be the middle of a big city, a futuristic space colony, Victorian England, a snow-bound country inn, etc.

Shifter – refers to a shape-shifter, an individual who is a human or humanoid, but can change into an animal or into a mythological or paranormal creature.

Short Novel – work that is longer than a novella, but shorter than a novel. Different publishers define a short novel by different word counts, but they are generally somewhere between 25,000 and 50,000 words.

Short Story – very short work of fiction that nonetheless tells a complete story. While precise definitions vary, short stories are generally considered to be those between about 1,000 and 10,000 words.

Show Don't Tell – possibly the most complex (and frustrating) concept in writing, this is a craft element that refers to demonstrating a character's inner feelings through dialog and action rather than simply telling the reader that, for example, "Mary is sad."

Signing – see book signing.

Silhouette – well-known romance imprint that was originally a part of Simon & Schuster and is now a part of Harlequin.

Simon & Schuster – one of the Big Six New York publishers.

Simultaneous Submission – can refer either to sending a submission to more than one publisher or agent at a time or to sending a submission to more than one editor at the same house (or agency) at the same time or to sending two separate submissions to the same entity at the same time. The first is quite common, but if you submit to several houses or agents and, you should let the other publishers know if and when you sign a contract so that they can remove your book from consideration. The second practice is heavily discouraged and will almost certainly irritate the recipients, possibly to the point of refusing to consider further submissions from you. The third varies by publisher. Some are quite willing to look at two or more books at once, but most prefer to evaluate one book at a time. Check the publisher's (or agent's) submission guidelines for details.

Single-author Anthology – see Anthology.

Single Title – book that is intended to stand alone rather than being a part of a series. This can apply to a series of books by the same author that have the same or overlapping characters, but can also refer to the broader term, such as series romance.

Slush Pile – the pile of as-yet unread (and usually unsolicited) manuscripts on an editor or agent's desk. Assume it's a large one.

Small Press – any press that isn't one of the Big Six or a well-known genre publisher, such as Harlequin, etc.

Special Call – when a publisher, usually a genre- or subgenre-specific publisher, puts out word that they are looking for submissions that follow a specific theme, usually to be published within a set period of time.

Special Interest Chapter – chapter of RWA that is based on genre or another element, rather than geography. Examples include the Fantasy, Fiction, and Paranormal chapter as well as Celtic Hearts and Passionate Ink.

Sprint – writing activity in which a writer races to complete a set number of words in a set period of time. Authors may sprint "together" with each working on his or her own project, to provide moral support and accountability.

Steampunk – subgenre, originally of science fiction, that postulates a historical world in which more modern technologies are available. Steampunk and steampunk elements now appear in romance, western, horror, fantasy, and many other genres.

Stock Signing – signing all the copies of your print book that a store has on hand, then returning them to the shelf for sale. Stock signings are usually best arranged in advance.

Story – group of elements that pertain to the storyline of your book and one part of the fiction triad (craft, story, and technical), the "story" is, of course, what you are telling when you write a book. Some consider "story" to include elements such as pacing, flow, and continuity. Others classify those elements as "craft," considering that "story" only refers to plot and the degree of completeness and entertainment provided by the tale.

Story Arc – the path your story takes throughout the life of the book. This includes all the events, as well as their effects on the characters. It might also refer to the path of a specific storyline or subplot, especially one that continues through multiple books (or movies or television shows).

Story Structure – the underlying organization of events in your story. Most stories begin with the setup, in which the reader meets the main characters and learns the basic premise of the book, then moves through several events or turning points, which escalate the story or action. The story peaks at the climax and wraps up with a denouement.

Stripped Book – print book that has had one or both of its covers removed in preparation of recycling, usually because of lack of sales. Stripped books are not supposed to be sold and neither authors nor publishers receive profits on them.

Strong Romantic Elements – book or novel that has strong elements of romance fiction, but is not actually a romance novel. This includes books focused on a love story that do not have a happy ending.

Style Guide – electronic or print manual that addresses common technical writing aspects such as punctuation, hyphenation, spelling choice, etc. Common styles include AP, which is used by the press, and CMOS, a modified version of which is used by many publishing houses. Those familiar with academic writing will most likely have used MLA, ALA, or APA to write papers and cite sources. Each house has its own style guide, which is the final word on all matters technical.

Subgenre – genre within a genre, such as <u>contemporary</u> romance, <u>cozy</u> mystery, <u>epic</u> fantasy, <u>vampire</u> paranormal, etc.

Submission – package, usually electronic nowadays, that you submit to a publisher or agent for consideration. This generally includes a partial or full of your manuscript, a query letter, and a synopsis. Always check the publisher or agent submission guidelines as they vary by entity.

Submission Guidelines – agent or publisher rules for submissions. These vary by publisher or agency and include items such as the amount of material to include, how long to wait for a response, where to send it, whether simultaneous submissions are accepted, formatting of your submission, etc. Most houses and agencies provide their guidelines on their websites or upon request.

Subplot – plot that occurs along with, but outside of, the primary plot. For example, a romance might focus on the development of a romantic relationship and have a subplot that involves reconciliation between the hero and his father.

Subplots might also involve secondary characters. Subplots should generally be wrapped up by the end of the book, unless they are intended to arc across two or more books in a series.

Subrights – see subsidiary rights.

Subsidiary Rights – rights to publish or produce a specific format of a book, such as paperback, audio, e-book, etc. Subsidiary rights may be negotiated separately or in combination.

Subsidy Publishing – varies slightly from vanity publishing in that the publisher maintains an imprint under which titles are published. The author, however, pays for (subsidizes) the cost of production.

Suspense – sometimes considered a subgenre of mystery, suspense is characterized by a fast pace and a suspenseful plot. It differs slightly from mystery in that the story is often told from dual perspectives: the "good guys" and the "bad guy." The reader often knows who the villain is—or at least what he's plotting. The suspense is created by wondering how (and whether) the good guys will stop the bad guy before he's able to carry out his nefarious plan.

Sweet – in romance, this generally refers to books in which the sexual interaction does not progress past kissing, though it may sometimes be used to indicate books in which any further sexual activity is strictly closed door. Note, however, that in erotic romance, "sweet" refers to a story involving a heterosexual couple in which there is no "kink" such as ménage or BDSM.

Synopsis – short document in which your basic plot points, character arcs, and story resolution are summarized to help an editor or agent decide whether to request or read the entire manuscript. Synopses are required with almost all submissions and contest entries. You will not enjoy composing this document. No one does. And it will only get marginally easier with time. Sorry. Welcome to the world of writing.

Tag – in publishing, this is a phrase or keyword associated with your book, such as "romance," "cowboys," "funny mysteries," or "vampires." These tags help potential readers find your books when they search for the kind of thing you write. Some online retailers allow readers (and sometimes authors) to tag books.

Tagging Party – party, usually virtual, in which several authors get together to tag one another's books on online retailer sites.

Tagline – sort of like a slogan, it's called a tagline because it is usually "tagged on" after the company (or author) name or logo. Authors, series, publishing houses, lines, and imprints may all have individual taglines.

Takedown Letter – letter, usually to a pirate site or individual website owner, advising them to remove your copyrighted material from their site.

Takedown Notice – see takedown letter.

TBR Pile (or stack or list) – stands for "to be read" pile. This is all those books you keep meaning to read, but haven't quite gotten to.

Technical – the mechanical part of writing: spelling, syntax, punctuation, sentence structure, etc.

Theme – an idea or concept central to your book. *Romeo and Juliet*, for example, includes themes such as "no one can escape fate" and "love leads to violence as easily as hate."

Third – usually refers to third person POV.

Third Party Retailer – anyone who sells your book, but is not your publisher. This includes online and brick-and-mortar booksellers and retailers.

Third Person – point of view in which the speaker is an unknown party outside the action, rather than one of the parties in the action. Many books are written in third person so the reader can see multiple perspectives. There are three forms of this perspective: third-person omniscient, third-person objective, and third-person limited. For new writers, telling them apart can be a bit of a challenge.

> E.g.: She walked toward the fountain, wondering if she could possibly be seeing her brother again.

Third Person Limited – perspective in which the author can talk only about the internal thoughts and feelings of a single character. He must demonstrate other characters' feelings through their actions and if the "feeling character" can't see it, neither can we.

Third Person Objective – third-person style in which no inner feelings or thoughts are revealed and the entire story is told through the action and dialog. Rarely used in narrative fiction, this concept is based on stageplay methodology, in which a character can only reveal her inner feelings by talking to herself or someone else.

Third Person Omniscient – perspective in which the author (and thereby the reader) has access to the inner thoughts and feelings of all characters simultaneously. This can get tricky to write without confusing the reader, and it is most commonly managed by alternating passages, scenes or chapters between one character's limited third and another (although some consider this "alternating limited third" rather than true third-person omniscient).

Third Wall – see breaking the third (or fourth) wall.

Thought Tag – sentence or phrase that precedes or follows a line of dialog and reveals the speaker's internal thoughts. Thought tags are often used to show a state of mind that conflicts with the speaker's actions. They are most often used in first-person POV. Depending on the publisher's house style, thought tags may or may not be italicized.

E.g.: "Sure, we can talk about it later." <u>Fat chance</u>.

Thriller – sometimes used interchangeably with suspense, thrillers are actually a bit more hardcore—somewhere between suspense and horror. Thrillers often feature human villains, such as serial killers, but may incorporate paranormal elements. Popular subgenres include legal, disaster, spy, and conspiracy.

Ticking Clock – situation in which something outside the character's control has created a critical timeline by which the story must resolve itself. This might be the time remaining until a bomb explodes or until the romantic hero is deployed overseas, etc. This element is used in most suspense and thriller novels, but can be used to great effect in just about any type of book.

Timeline – time across which your book occurs. This can be anything from a few minutes or hours to decades.

Time Travel – a specific subgenre, usually, but not always, of Sci-Fi, that involves someone from one time period going backward or forward in time. This differs from futuristic or historical, which are set entirely in, and feature characters exclusively from, the designated time period.

Tone – the overall feel of your writing. It might be funny, irreverent, bleak, refined, Southern, European, etc.

Too Stupid To Live – this is the character, usually a heroine, for whom the reader feels little sympathy because she keeps putting herself in harm's way for no apparent valid reason. This is the heroine who runs up the stairs instead of through the open front door when the killer is chasing her (unless, of course, she keeps a .44 in her bedside table) or the one who slips past the police protecting her home and wanders alone into the woods "to think about things."

TPB – stands for trade paperback.

Trademark – any mark (logo, tagline, etc.) you own, either by right of commerce or by copyright. You don't have to register a mark with the trademark office in order to prove you own it, but the burden of proof of ownership is far more intense if you don't.

Traditional Publishing – refers to the model of publishing that was the standard for most of publishing history (and the only option, for much of it). This model involves selling a book to one of the Big Six (usually through an agent), then having it appear in print via print runs rather than POD. At one time, books came out in hardback first, then in paperback. Now, many skip the hardback stage and eventually come out in e-book. Some traditional publishers are even experimenting with simultaneous digital releases.

Trade Paperback – in publishing, this refers to the higher-quality paperbacks available in bookstores (as opposed to mass market paperbacks). Note that, in the comic book world, a trade paperback is a book that reprints several issues of a comic series into one bound edition.

Trope – in literature, a trope is a well-known (and usually popular) basis for a storyline. In romance, this might be friends-to-lovers or boss-and-secretary. In mystery it might be the-butler-did-it or the closed-door-murder. Sci-Fi or urban fantasy might use rebels-overthrow-evil-empire or alien-trapped-on-earth. You get the picture. Every genre has them.

TSTL – see too stupid to live.

Turnaround Time – time during which some deliverable is completed. This usually refers to a publisher or agent's response time, but can also mean the time between submitting a request for cover art and receiving the art, etc.

Turning Point – point at which a story or a character's emotional journey, takes a turn—either for the better or the worse.

TwitFic – fiction told in one, or a series of, Twitter posts—140 characters at a time. Yeah, that's what I said. But people do it. And love it.

Unagented – author who does not have an agent representing his work. Some publishers accept "unagented submissions" while others do not.

Unearned – when the amount of your royalties on sales fails to meet the amount of your advance.

Unresolved Sexual Tension – sexual tension between romantic partners that has not yet found an outlet. In sweet romance, this outlet will be a kiss. In other types of romance, it may be a kiss, sex, or anything in between. Unresolved sexual tension can serve to increase reader anticipation, but must be managed carefully so that readers don't become frustrated.

Unshifted – term for a shape-shifter that is currently in human form.

Unsolicited – unasked-for. If you send an unsolicited query, it means that the editor or agent has not asked you to do so. Most submissions happen this way, but some editors and agents do not accept unsolicited queries or manuscripts, so be sure to check the submission guidelines first.

Upon Acceptance – when you and your publisher sign the contract for your book.

Upon Delivery – this can mean two things, and may be qualified in your contract. It may mean upon delivery of a manuscript that was accepted on proposal. It can also mean upon delivery of a final, fully-edited manuscript.

Upon Publication – once your book is published and available for purchase. Certain portions of an advance may be payable at this point, depending on your contract terms.

Urban Fantasy – fiction genre that is set in an urban (city) environment and has strong fantasy and/or paranormal elements. These stories are usually somewhat grittier than traditional fantasy novels and are often set in dystopian environments.

Vanity Press – press, usually print, that prints your books for a flat or graduated fee. This differs from self-publishing, in which you set up your books for electronic or print distribution and share the sales monies with the press. Before the self-publishing revolution, vanity publishing was sometimes the only way to see your name in print if none of the traditional houses would publish your book. Within the writing community, vanity publishing is generally considered questionable, particularly now that so many other options are available.

Variable-width Serif Font – the gold standard of fonts for submissions (and printing, in general), though some publishers will also take monotype serif fonts. A serif font is one with serifs (the little "doodads" at the end of each stroke of each letter). For example, the tiny cross-bar at the bottom of letters such as "A," or "F." A sans serif font literally means a font without serifs (doodads). A variable-width font is one in which different letters have different widths (the "w" is wider than the "I," for example). This contrasts with a monospace font, in which all the letters have the same width. So, a variable-width serif font is one in which the letters are different widths and have serifs.

Voice – the distinctive way in which an author or character talks (or writes). It includes a wide range of characteristics such as use of slang, word choice, sentence structure, tone, syntax, etc. As a writer, you will eventually develop your own voice, unique to you and based on your personality, background, and individual style.

Weak Vessel – character, usually female, who can't do anything without help and is unfulfilled without a man. Not a reader favorite.

Web Store – online store, usually operated by a publisher or author.

Western – stories set in the American plains (or, occasionally, an equivalent, such as an Australian cattle ranch). While any story can be set in, say, Wyoming, westerns tend to be more focused on the land and culture than on a romance or mystery (although western is also a recognized subgenre of both of these genres). Subgenres include revenge, lawmen, pioneer or settler, and buffalo soldier.

WIP – stands for work in progress. This is a book or story you're working to prepare for submission.

Women's Fiction – genre of fiction that deals primarily with women's issues and relationships. Romance and chick lit are sometimes considered a part of women's fiction, but the subgenre actually has a fairly distinct readership and tone. Women's fiction often focuses on relationships other than romantic ones, such as siblings, mother-daughter relations, friendships, etc.

Word Choice – editor's note that means you might want to consider using another word. Often written as "w/c."

Word Count – number of words in a story or book. This is how book lengths are measured in the publishing industry (as opposed to page counts, which is what a reader typically looks at).

Workshop – short class on a writing or publishing topic. Workshops might last for an hour or a couple of days, depending on the intensity and they are a major focus of most writers' conferences.

World – the environment in which your characters live. Most people think of this in terms of fantasy or sci-fi, but if you make up a subdivision or town that your characters live in, you've built a world. Note that worlds also encompass the people, streets, businesses, and other elements. Worlds can also be reality-based; you might easily set a story in a made-up neighborhood in San Francisco or Hawaii.

World Building – the act of creating a world for your characters to live in.

Writer – person who writes. This is also you.

Writer Conference (or Convention) – conference (or convention) focused on writers, the publishing industry, and the craft of writing. Main functions typically include workshops, pitch appointments, and networking times.

Writer/Reader Conference (or Convention) – conference (or convention) intended to bring readers and writers together. These conferences usually do include workshops, but the topics are usually of interest to both audiences. Mixers, book signings, meet and greets, author Q&As, parties, and other opportunities for interaction are also a key part of such conferences.

Writer's Block – when you can't think of what to write next or how to make a scene work out. There are entire articles and books devoted to moving past writer's block. If this is a recurring issue for you, you might want to check a few out and try some different strategies.

Writer's Market – print and electronic publication that lists editors, agents, magazines, and other publication opportunities, along with brief submission information. Writer's Market also publishes a series of writing books.

Writer Voice – see voice.

Writing Contest – see contest

Writing Process – your personal approach to getting the story down and refined. Some authors create a written outline, others advance plan in their heads, others wing it. Some authors listen to mood music, others prefer silence. Some read or watch films to get in the right mindset. There is no "right" way and there are as many processes as there are writers. You'll find and develop yours as you go.

Writing Prompt – picture, phrase, or set of words or objects designed to prompt a story or thought. The idea is to get your creative juices flowing and get you writing.

YA – see Young Adult

Young Adult – fiction genre (and also a subgenre of romance) for which the primary target reader is an adolescent or teen. Various sources define the age group as somewhere between 14 and 21. Young adult novels generally feature protagonists in the same age range who are dealing with typical teenage emotions. Note, however, that a book featuring a teenaged protagonist is not necessarily a Young Adult novel; stories with very adult themes sometimes feature non-adult main characters.

About the Author

Maggie is an author, speaker, marketing strategist, freelance writer, and future professor. She's also a reader, life learner, dog schmuck, hair flower obsessionist, foodie, and dreamer. During her 20-year career, she's drafted literally hundreds of process manuals, press releases, how-tos, business plans, and lifestyle and career articles, as well as two textbooks and several award-winning marketing pieces, ads, and video scripts. She's published award-winning light erotic romance as Maggie Montgomery and is working on her first romantic suspense as Maggie Washington. She'd also like to publish in comedic and middle grades mystery, children's literature, and horror. Maggie is a member of RWA, Georgia Romance Writers, Passionate Ink, and MENSA. In April 2013, she launched a series of short reference guides, Writer's Bites: Topics You Can Sink Your Teeth Into, beginning with Writing & Publishing Terminology and Writing & Publishing Terminology for Romance Writers. She lives in metro-Atlanta's "Southern Crescent" with her husband and their four-legged kid, a black lab/German Shepherd mix named Rowdy. Connect at maggieworth.com, find her on Twitter as MaggieSheWrote, or visit her blog at FiveforFiction.com.

www.ingramcontent.com/pod-product-compliance
Lightning Source LLC
Chambersburg PA
CBHW070701290526
45790CB00001B/403